JOURN  E
HEAI S

exploring spiritual practices
of Quaker worship

edited by
Elizabeth Brown
Alec Davison

Booklet 1: a publication of
The Kindlers

In this series:

Breakthrough to Unity *(2010)*
The Power we Call God *(2011)*
Answering that of God *(2012)*
Love Growing in Us *(2012)*

Published in 2009 in the United Kingdom by
The Kindlers, a project of North West London
Area Quaker Meeting, Britain Yearly Meeting,
of the Religious Society of Friends (Quakers)

Study Guide with booklist, for groups wishing
to work together on this text, available from the
above address:
£3.00 + £1.00 p&p. (cheque to *The Kindlers*)

ISBN: 978-0-9562245-0-7

Financed by the Joyce Green Association.

1st printing 2009:   1,000 copies
2nd printing 2010:   1,000 copies
3rd printing 2012:   1,000 copies

Preface

A long time ago, it is reputed that a worthy Quaker elder ministered in Meeting, following a hectic week of barn-storming mission, "O, Lord, if any glimmering of grace has been kindled by these humble endeavours, we pray thee to water that spark!"

This booklet is the first published glimmering of a new-born, informal Quaker group, The Kindlers, and its anxious incendiaries are hoping for a gentle wafting of welcome rather than a wholesale watering. The spark is a response to the new Quaker five-year plan, 'A framework for action, 2009–2014 *Together in worship and witness*'. In that challenging document Friends are encouraged to be innovative and entrepreneurial in addressing seven priorities in the life of the Society today.

The foremost of these is to 'Strengthen the spiritual roots in our meetings and in ourselves'. "We need kindlers not snuffers," is the cry; "more pro-action, less institutional thwarting." The work of The Kindlers is an engagement with that summons. But it raises a profound question for Quakers: how can the worshipping life of the Society be renewed within a religious faith that eschews leadership and gurus, has no paid ministry and can claim little contemporary inspiring spiritual literature?

It can only come from the grass-roots, for there is no top-down. The person in the pew is as good as it gets. Our most helpful recent model is that of our sister organisation, Quaker Quest, also a project of North West London Area Meeting. From a committed experiment over eight years in one particular situation, a team of Friends who felt they were acting under concern, evolved experimentally a pattern of working, developed a way of training others and then travelled throughout Britain Yearly Meeting and abroad to help local Meetings set up their own Quaker Quests.

Just as their concern with outreach also proved to be a most beguiling form of inreach, so it is hoped that The Kindlers' overt concern with inreach will become a telling form of outreach.

Introduction

Quaker worship is the heart of the Quaker Way. Historically many early Friends of Truth died in prison for the freedom to practise this new form of communal contemplation. Just as a country's heartland is the vitally important territory lying at its centre, so the spiritual heartland of all Quaker life is the unique, precious and amazing experience of direct resonance with the Divine: our worship. Quakers are essentially mystics, as well as prophets.

This form of identifying with the sacredness of all life, our worship, through silence, stillness and words spoken from the heart, is an exciting discovery for contemporary seekers. "Just what I've been looking for." "Help me more." "I want to go deeper." "What do I do now?"

Newcomers are, however, often innocent of any previous mature experience of worship, or are refugees from ways that no longer speak to them. At the same time there are long-standing Friends whose spiritual practice has not kept up with the shifts in understandings of our social consciousness today, or whose heartland at the moment is a dry and barren place. Both seekers and members are searching for soul-food, for the spiritual nourishment only gleaned by sinking into the Source that is always waiting in our depths. How to find such nurture is the quest.

The Kindlers' programmes are exploring ways to help. While open to all Friends, they are especially aimed at elders and mentors of a Meeting's spiritual life. Through group-work and personal engagement participants look again at the whole process of our regular Meetings for Worship and together seek to enrich the spiritual practices of that process.

This booklet allows Kindler participants to speak of their experience. It is a collection of their responses gathered to help others. The first part tells of a Meeting for Worship in its totality, through a range of voices. The following eight sections pursue the narrative of the spiritual practices that make up the unity of that worship experience.

Experiencing Worship

Quakers come together in Sunday worship for every kind of human need: to express our gratitude for the gifts of life; to celebrate and share our joys; to acknowledge our grief and hurt, failures and disappointments; to be part of endeavours to help those suffering or facing injustice; to find meaning and to have purpose strengthened. Essentially we come to be with a warm-hearted group of exploring Friends, who together will evoke a unique silent stillness through which we can be in touch with the deepest we know.

Quakers have called this the Divine, the Light, Truth, Reality, Presence, the Source, even God. But this is no God made in our image, of punishment and guilt, it is a healing Power, a creative Energy that has birthed us and totally accepts us, unfolding an abundance of life for us, desiring we should be made whole. The Power is as intimate to us as breath and blood: it is as intrinsically within us as we, and all things, are within its embrace. The dynamic of the worshipping group makes that real, for in the Meeting's processes of centring down there is drawn out of us a giving to the others as they are giving to us. As a community we are spiritually entangled beyond the place where any individualistic meditation might reach. For each of us it is different; we emerge nourished, rested, perhaps provoked, often changed. We will have known 'the promptings of truth and love'.

Yet for all our unique experiences, there is a pattern, a path in our journey through the heartlands, as these voices tell.

★ Terminal illness within my family is difficult to bear without getting cynical about a so-called God of love. So my spiritual practice in the weeks between Meetings has become a growing mindfulness that can centre on absolutely anything ~ to find grace and beauty and wonder within it. This may be in food I prepare or eat, the objects of my home, what I can see through windows, or the never-ending change of everything in the garden: skies, birds, insects, plants. As I lose love through oncoming death I seem to be finding it in the world around me.

★ On Sunday morning I try to get up in good time and in between a light breakfast and seeing who else is coming to Meeting, take some time away for ten minutes to read and reflect on a passage, often from *Quaker Faith and Practice*. If possible we don't do any housework or chores and leave in good time. Whether by car or bus I attempt to listen attentively to any companion, but not to get too involved in conversation; they usually sense, if I don't say, that I'm trying to travel quietly. A town Meeting House, ours is a very early one and I always have a sense of the thousands of Friends who have walked up the path to be greeted by a friendly doorkeeper over some hundreds of years. It's often not easy, but apart from greeting different Friends while taking off coats, I avoid getting involved with arrangements for events, or news and chatter. Frequently I'm one of the first to be in the Meeting room itself, taking a different seat each time, which seems to make a great difference to the awareness of community. I like to help the other Friends there create the silence to welcome those who come.

★ Jumping off the deep end into the pool of silence is how I used to do it, but I slowly realized that I wasn't taking my body with me, which was making its own demands. So for the first ten minutes now I've developed my own practices. From feet to head I go through every part, relaxing it and easing away tensions, and often while doing this gently smiling at those still arriving. This leads into an awareness of my breathing, which I'm now able to slow down as I say a mantra in my head, often 'Be still and know that I am God'. The quietening body helps my mind to slow down, but it's still often distracted. Rather than fight it, I let the thoughts pass by, like clouds, not engaging with them, or letting them fall like stones in water. It's difficult. But it helps me sink into prayer.

★ Silence is my great easing from the pressures and busyness of the week. I feel as if I can just throw all my problems into the centre of the Meeting with a "There, you deal with them." Let me be free! Let me swing in this hammock of release! Birds outside prompt me into prayers of thankfulness for beauty and wonder in the world, for blessings of my life, for family and friends, and the good things I've enjoyed this week. This act of gratitude opens me; I expand into it and feel a healing of Spirit. It leads me to pray for those close to me who are troubled, or others I've seen on the news and been disturbed by. Then my own needs inevitably swim to the surface. The power of the stillness works at them.

★ It's a slow letting-go process of unwinding, centring, spilling out my cares to be embraced not by a nothing, but by a strange something. At times the silence is palpable. When I have been able to be really spiritually alert, awake and attentive, I have known a feeling of being held, touched by the Presence. Occasionally, I have lost myself in the essence of my contemplation, whether centred on another or on Jesus or on an anxiety. Time has stood still: I have been here and not here, held in the moment, now. It is a rare time, beyond waiting, of being given. This is my closest to standing in the Light; an absolute moment of grace. I've found it disturbing and its implications are with me for the following week.

★ Very occasionally I've found myself on my feet giving ministry and then I can barely remember what I said. It has been sudden. I've felt a glimpse of an insight and been weighing up whether this is just for me or for the Meeting, when my body has precipitated me to stand and I just have to give myself to my trembling tongue. It's weird, but often when I've been thinking whether to minister or not, someone else has stood up and said something better along the lines of what I was going to say. Ministry doesn't always speak to me: then I struggle to hear the words behind words. But there are Friends who speak from profound depths and I relish and remember the authenticity of what they have shared.

★ Later on in the hour the silence seems to gather weight and become 'heavy'; like wading through thick mud or groping through dense mist, but without getting stuck or lost. This is what, for me, the 'gathered' Meeting is: when everyone's thought and focus seem to be settled, concentrated, perhaps pointing the same way. We may all be contemplating different things, but we seem to have a common direction in the 'heavy' silence. If everyone knows that something momentous has occurred in the world, such as some dreadful accident or terrorist attack, or if there's been a death in the Meeting, then you can literally feel the weight of common thought: it seems almost tangible. Perhaps you could even say that this is really all one thought. We are one.

★ In our Meeting the children come in at the end and join us to listen to Afterword, which an elder introduces. Here anyone is invited to share what might have been on their tongue-tip to minister, or to ask about or to share any aspect of the worship experience. This is tenderly done and often takes us into new thinking, encouraging newcomers to speak who might have been too shy before. In shaking hands then, to conclude, we seem more of a united community. While notices don't appeal to everyone, I'm always impressed by the range of involvements the Meeting has and the host of events we are being invited to. It seems a big, nation-wide family. Refreshments afterwards and a chance to chat to new attenders are really welcome.

★ There's never a week when inbetween-whiles I am not involved in one of the Meeting's committees, usually in somebody's home. We try to arrange that everyone in the Meeting is on at least one committee. It's our traditional way of ensuring that we all feel part of things and begin to understand how we run by mutual responsibility. But as well as feeling energised by the worship, I find it all too frequently prods me into doing something about engaging with the ways of change in the world at large ~ for me in environmental issues. The Quaker way is essentially a way of life.

Being a Quaker is not a one-day-a-week affair. It's an every-day lifestyle lived in the spirit of Jesus, from whose teachings Friends evolved our essential Quaker values and testimonies. For more than three hundred years they have been shown to work amazingly well in practice for the universal good. But they need careful nourishment; Sunday worship only really flourishes when our spiritual life is well-tended ground. A century ago this would have been primarily through daily family prayers and Bible reading. Today, especially where only one parent may be a Quaker and many of us will have come from non-Christian backgrounds, our spiritual practices will be highly varied and we each need to find those that speak to our particular condition.

The aim is to affirm the sacred in whatever we do. There is no part of our mundane reality that is not irradiated with divinity, but in the hourly stress and busyness of coping with a multitude of tasks, the sense of holiness and wholeness inevitably gets swamped. The disciplines of daily and weekly practices help us to hold on to the inward dimension of life, come what may. Though it is best if these practices are not followed too obsessively, becoming duty rather than enjoyment, yet a degree of discipline is necessary as other priorities soon overwhelm.

What we choose to do is highly personal and depends on what makes for a balanced life. Those engaged in work of considerable thinking may need a practice of bodily expression; others, highly involved in things physical, can be helped by something more reflective; but everyone needs to find space just to 'be' and times of silence. Spirituality is no longer seen as just solemn moments about things 'religious' or bouts of piety and self-righteousness: joy, fun, celebration, creativity and gratitude are essentially enlargements of Spirit.

At heart the practice will be about focus, about mindfulness, about giving our full attention, often to small things. Then the spiritual can be seen as when we lose our 'ego' in an 'other', which is nourishing and healthy; when we let go of our self-will to be at one with the greater Self, the Light. Early Friends knew the parable of Jesus as 'Divine wedge', from medieval WEDCH, originally plough, then carpenter's tool, which would firmly keep the door of our heart ajar for the openings and enlargements of the Spirit to enter. We might see this holy W.E.D.C.H. as the Worship, Empathy, Discernment, Creativity and Healing, that are the five gateways of Friends' everyday spiritual practices today.

1. WORSHIP: *being open to the sacramental vision*

★ I give myself some minutes on first waking up to feel thankfulness for being alive and all the blessings of the day.

★ Before seeing a difficult client at work, or facing a task I dread, I give myself two minutes of stillness.

★ Just to be able to spend five minutes during the day sitting and emptying myself makes all the difference. At other times I just daydream, or enter into a fantasy world and it's good. Often I make time, pledging with myself to watch less TV.

★ I try to set aside a daily time for reflection, pondering over a poem from an anthology, or short Bible reading, or an extract from a book of quotations, like *Quaker Faith and Practice* or *The Perennial Philosophy*, or a book of paintings or photographs.

★ At the end of the day I give thanks for it and review what has happened, especially the unexpected things and the questions that arose. Then I put them into a 'space' before sleep. On awakening I'm often given the answers.

★ Our Meeting encourages those in the same overseer's group to come together in someone's house once a month, for a go-round, time for questions, then worship-sharing.

★ We have mid-week evening worship, when more of the young people come, and it feels very different from Sundays.

★ Our *Experiment with Light* group is always open to newcomers, so it keeps it fresh. It has really helped to deepen the worshipping life of the Meeting.

★ At home we've started saying grace before meals again.

★ For some years our interfaith group just used to have talks and questions with people from other faiths. Now we've developed enough mutual trust for practitioners to lead us in the spiritual practices of their faith: we've fasted, we've chanted, we've meditated. It's brought us more together.

★ I'm part of a non-Quaker workshop group evolving its own rituals and ceremonies for special community and family occasions to give them more significance. We've had some profound experiences that feel oddly Quakerly.

★ I find walking mindfully in town or country very powerful.

★ Whether in the garden or a park, just to be still and contemplate anything at all is increasingly precious to me: plants, trees, flowers, moving water, birds, insects, animals.

★ Hands deep in soil, planting or weeding or watering in my bit of a garden, transforms me. It's now one of the deepest spiritual experiences I know.

2. *EMPATHY: love, friendship, relationships, compassion*

★ When I've given myself totally, listening with undivided attention to someone I've met casually in a bus or a train, in a post-office queue or a café, it's invariably led to an unforgettable fusing for both of us. Something happens that opens me up.

★ We asked around in our group and over half were involved in a weekly volunteering session with Samaritans, or an Oxfam shop, in a youth club or with school reading, and prison or hospital visiting. It seemed that at the heart of this work was listening in depth to other people's stories. We felt that for everyone there's a profound spiritual need for respect and affirmation.

3. *DISCERNMENT: from head knowledge to heart wisdom*

★ I find depth in reading a few pages of non-fiction a day about something new to me and then contemplating them.

★ In recent years I've gone back to reading the best of today's children's novels: they're often full of the spiritual.

★ I've kept a dream diary for many years. Learning about the symbols revealed helps me to read other spiritual works.

★ My daily spiritual journal is a mixture of reflections, insights, quotations, character sketches, short poems, haikus.

★ I challenge myself to make going shopping more spiritual: choices, quantities, where from, who made, great gratitude.

4. *CREATIVITY: processes of making things new*

★ Playing my flute with great mindfulness or listening to music with absolute attentiveness brings me infinite richness.

★ I see my painting as an act of prayer. It's a process of entering deep inside whatever it is that the paint is describing.

★ Singing a great oratorio chorus, with everyone spilling their heart out, is the nearest I think I'll ever get to Heaven on Earth.

★ Through our dance improvisation to music group, I'm taken to another dimension of being. It's absolutely mystical.

★ Nothing's more spiritually exhilarating to me than seeing what appears when my craft-medium and imagination go free.

5. *HEALING: body and mind, caring, reconciliation*

★ I feel whole again when I indulge in my week's speciality bath, with ample time and lots of lotions to banish the stress.

★ Sport is my salving and whether it's gym-work, running or swimming, I can now focus in the 'being' beyond the 'action'.

★ Once a week we both share in mindfully preparing a meal together and then ritualistically relish it as we eat and drink.

★ I'm comfortable with sex as spiritual, when we take time being tender, experiment in foreplay, find depth in passion.

★ It's wonderful when the 'magic moment' happens in a neighbourhood dispute at my local council mediation centre.

Crossing Thresholds

Many Quakers hold that all life is one and that all life is sacred. It has a unity and integrity to it that science increasingly affirms, as it demonstrates the interconnectedness and interdependency of everything. Yet, all things are unique and for humanity, founded as we are on our emotions, things *feel* different and we discern them differently. Things are not the same: they are not uniform. Think of Friday evenings and Monday mornings; or of the first and last day of a holiday. Buildings all have their characteristic auras and atmospheres. Nature is breathtakingly beautiful or disturbingly repellent. People are a bunch of friendly or malevolent personalities, and we each veer between a range of consciousnesses from asleep to wide awake, or day-dream-fantasy to drugged. We move from one state of mind, or building, or group of friends to another and we adapt and change in the process. If we are honest, some things or situations seem more sacred than others. This is so with each of us in our engagements with acts of worship.

We may say that we could worship anywhere, and we could, but on Sundays we don't. We usually go to our regular local Meeting House. We may say that all days are equally sacred and we can worship at any time, and in many ways we might, yet most of us come together at a set time on Sundays. Once we set buildings, space, time, days and states of mind apart then in our consciousness, and especially in our unconscious, we will make personal, often unaware, rituals to move from one state to another, to overcome barriers and negotiate boundaries in order to *transcend* the secular, to touch the holy. Glimpses of transcendence may be given to us by grace. For this we have first to cross thresholds. Becoming aware of this universal process and acknowledging the transitions is an early stage in the deepening process of worship.

★ To go or not to go to Meeting? In deciding to go it seems to me that I've crossed the first threshold and I ask myself if that's the moment when Meeting really begins? For aren't I, like any seeker, someone who really knows that there is something to find? Don't I only wait in the Light because I know that there is something to wait for? The body knows long before the mind. We are urged to come 'with heart and mind prepared' and I now feel that while the heart should be open, it doesn't mean that the mind should be empty; it needs to be appropriately nourished. For each of us is also enjoined to 'yield yourself and all your outward concerns to God's guidance'. In our tradition God is a reality, a focus, a source of inspiration to which we will give up our 'selves'.

★ Journeys of all kinds have their own resonance and transitions. I become aware of my movement from the secular towards the sacred. The quest-like lure is my 'openness to the possibilities of the Meeting'. (George Gorman) In responding there is a leaving; an intention to engage when most neighbours don't, so the ambivalence of going against the social grain; there are fellow-journeyers, means of transport, incidents and provocations, anxieties about time, and, eventually, arrival. A lot has been going on and my spirit needs to catch up. Anticipated silence and stillness become more urgent. Consciousness shifts.

★ I slow down for the actual threshold of the Meeting House and attempt to make crossing it a conscious act. Ours is not an old building, yet it is part of a longer tradition and symbolically the path is well-worn. Worshippers are not alone, but part of a fellow-ship: I instantly warm to familiarity and friendship. At times when I am doorkeeper I have wondered if the welcoming, shaking of hands is not a sacred act: it's certainly a precious human act. The doorkeeper in our rural Meeting is always first in, unlocks, prepares the Meeting room and its table: so is host. Doorkeepers in myths are guardians, too: our realm of silence needs preserving from chatter and disturbance; so just brief greetings and coats off.

★ From the lobby I move to the Meeting room itself, in our case with an overseer at its door. We will be given a smile of recognition, maybe a mouthed "welcome", but no words to disturb the other side. The swish of the door is carefully managed, a gentle indication invites me in and over the last physical threshold. Here the boundary is as much a spiritual one. In all manner of subtle ways this has been prepared for. I have now moved from worldly into sacred space dedicated at this time to God; from idle speech to revered silence; from complexity to simplicity; from rank and class to equality in the spirit; from conditional merits to unconditional acceptance. We now all become Quaker ministers.

★ Standing on the other side of the last door I often feel a qualm of exposure. Because there is no 'front' somewhere at the other end and a 'back' one can slip into, it feels a bit like the universe, where everything is a centre point and there is no edge. Chairs or benches are in circles, radiating out in rows from a table with no key chairs for top people. Everybody sits where they want, some roughly where they have often sat (my wife) and others choosing somewhere different each time (me)! Fixed benches are from days when Friends were more united in beliefs; individual chairs reflect today's greater diversity. The silence is already deep, for it begins when the first Friend arrives and some come early to help centre it.

★ There is a visual threshold yet to cross. A newcomer soon registers that our Quaker Meeting House, in its simplicity, is visually as well as aurally silent. The walls are still; colours subdued, and there is no busyness of ornamentation or decoration. Even in old buildings, like ours, there are no memorials for the dead, Biblical texts or religious symbols. In place of a font or pulpit there can be a central table, with a vase of flowers, the Bible, Quaker texts and today, maybe, an interfaith text. Some Meetings encourage their children once a month to put alternatives to flowers – earth, water, stones, fossils, fruits, candles, toys, food. Some table-less Meetings scatter books on seats, creating 'empty' central space.

★ I've recently started to stand in the shoes of new seekers and imagine how they see us and our Meeting Houses. It's a telling psychological threshold. I know my inner being is deeply shaped by context and that there are good studies now about 'Architecture and Spirit', not just the religious. Some of our Quaker worship spaces have a stunning beauty in the simple austerity of natural materials: others are depressingly utilitarian and domestic, "somewhere you go for afternoon tea but find no tea" ~ nor even any soul-lifting. As we move to renovate and rebuild in the light of sustainability and carbon foot-printing we have a unique opportunity to catch ideas from university interfaith chapels, James Turrell skyscapes and meditation domes creating a network of Quaker centres to face the challenges ahead. The heart of each could be a simple community sanctuary of breathtaking inspiration.

★ Ours is a middle-to-large inner city Meeting with a shifting membership. There have been many deaths of older Friends, but an even greater regular flow of newcomers, including young adults and families, from our work in Quaker Week and Quaker Quest. Now we have not only successfully introduced Afterword at the end of the worship hour but also Beforeword at the start of it. Here an elder stands, welcomes everyone and introduces and reads either an extract from or from what the elders have themselves written, about our manner of worship: silence and stillness, waiting in the Light, ministry and more.

★ As Meeting begins I am led through the window before me to the Scottish hills beyond. "Have I come", I ask, "to the threshold of Meeting prepared to give up certain assumptions, to suspend disbelief, to entertain the possibility that thoughts, feelings, ideas and experiences may be created and rendered differently? Do I stand in humility?" as Isaac Pennington asked in 1658:

> …letting go of our cramped grip on our defences is to 'get low'. This means letting go of our controlling so as to sense the presence and guidance of the Divine; moreover it breeds an attentiveness to 'the day of small things', to the small concrete matters in our lives.

Centring Down

I once visited a 200-mile-long Mammoth Cave in Kentucky and felt as though I was entering a small bit of the Earth's centre, which heats all life on our planet. Centring down will lead us to our 'cave of the heart', or core, where our fire of love resides. As we live from this centre we are kindled with passion for life and its Creator. We, too, want to create life anew, within us and without. We can intentionally focus or centre on our Divine core using 'aids' that can be laid aside once we've achieved that place of contemplation that we desire in Meeting for Worship.

When amongst the circle of worshippers, we could be compared to spokes of a wheel, with God as the centre, so that the nearer we are to God, the nearer we are to each other, thus we become gathered to God in the silence.

To centre down we first need to still our bodies and then our wandering thoughts. Whatever we did in preparation for coming to Meeting can help or hinder this process. Do we come with heart and mind prepared?

★ At home I draw a mandala, when I feel 'all over the place'. It helps me to come 'home' to my centre. I re-collect myself. A mandala can be created in any media and I build it up from the centre. It is a circle or square that is made up of patterns, shapes and colours that can remind me of the wholeness of life in unity with God, for the many parts make up the whole. It can be used as a vehicle for meditation, for it has a calming and healing effect that increases a sense of balance and proportion.

★ I ground myself in the place where I am worshipping, be it a community hall, street corner or Meeting House, as the sacred and the secular are one before God.

★ Certain places hold stunning silence, like old Meeting Houses that have known much prayer. I'm helping to create that.

CENTRING THE BODY: *releasing tensions*

★ I like to sit in the same place each week. It helps me settle.

★ I relax my body, de-tensing myself from toes to head and seat my back and bottom well into the chair, then with an upright back and hands loose on my lap and my feet firmly 'earthed' on the floor I attend to slowing down my breath.

★ I concentrate on feeling full as I take an in breath and count to three, then empty myself in letting go with my out breath to a count of three, then increase the count to four, then five, then relax and breathe normally. This stills me.

Thich Nhat Hanh (a Vietnamese Buddhist monk) suggests following one's breath, simply saying to oneself "Breathing in I calm my body. Breathing out I smile." This deepens my breathing, which enables relaxation, whilst being spiritually alert.

★ My Meeting lets me lie down on the floor, which I appreciate.

★ I concentrate on my chakras (energy centres), especially the sacral area below my umbilicus as my body's centre: it's sometimes called the 'seat of compassion'.

★ If you wonder what to do with your hands during worship you might like to consider this exercise. Place your hands palms down as a symbolic indication of your desire to turn over your concerns to God. After a time of surrender turn your palms up as a sign that you are ready to receive: then rest in the silence.

CENTRING ON THE OTHER: *connecting*

★ I send love to those entering Meeting for Worship.

★ I think of all those present as well as those who are absent, ill or travelling.

★ I remember those who have worshipped here in the past. They have helped to make this a sacred space.

★ I feel excitement at the possibility I may be changed. May I be filled with God's love for all? Each of us has within a Divine centre, where 'Truth abides in fullness'. (H. T. Hamblin) I wish to keep in constant touch with this as it brings great peace.

CENTRING THE MIND: passing over thoughts

★ I have a ' monkey mind' full of thoughts. I say a silent mantra: "Shalom, Haverim" (Peace, Friend) or the Lord's Prayer. I repeat it with my in-and-outbreaths for a few times then let it go, but resume saying it if my thoughts begin to intrude. This practice calms me. The word 'mantra' is borrowed from the Hindu tradition, where a word, phrase or sentence is addressed to, or describes Divinity. I test what is an appropriate mantra for me, so that I can live intimately with it and admit it deep into my heart. It doesn't need to be spoken out loud.

★ I acknowledge my worries and anchor them to consider later.

★ I drop my 'stones of thought' into the deep water of silence. The ripples slowly cease. I'm eased and centred.

★ I'm told that my heart's centre is where my treasure lies. Sometimes I need to dig, but at other times I find 'the pearl of great price' (Matt 13: 46) just lying there! What joy!

★ I picture the sky-like nature of my mind with thoughts passing by as if they are clouds and try not to become attached to them.

★ My centring image is of a lake with boats sailing on it, blown gently by the wind. I feel lulled into the quietness.

★ Mine is of a large bowl and I and others at Meeting are gradually sliding down into the centre, where we settle.

★ I dive off a diving board into the deep of silence.

★ I visualise myself on a seashore hearing the trickling of waves over pebbles and this stills me.

★ I brush off my cares like falling leaves, or they take flight like birds on the wing. I then rest in safety.

★ I hear music in the air, or listen to birdsong and church bells, which connect me to all within the Meeting and without.

★ The vista of blue carpet calms me and I stop thinking and then enter a state of 'calm abiding'. (Buddhist phrase)

★ I use a Buddhist image of myself as a block of ice or slab of butter sitting in the sun, or presence, of Divine love and melting.

CENTRING IN DEPTH: *sinking down*

★ I go downwards and inwards; upwards and outwards. I am reaching into the core of myself, where 'the seed of God' resides.

★ Gradually I begin to feel myself receiving love in the silence and a huge gratitude wells up in me that nourishes my dry, thirsty inner landscape. I feel great thankfulness for life, adoration for my Maker and praise for the fountain of goodness that springs forth from this centre. I enter a blessed state like the Cistercian monks who saw centring prayer as a prelude to the openness of contemplative prayer, when we are 'looking at God, who is ever present, and letting him look on us'. (Gerhard Tersteegan)

★ I centre myself by recalling one of Meister Eckhart's sermons, as a passage from one of them already starts a Meeting for Worship for me, wherever I am.

★ I enter a meditative state, lost to myself, maybe falling asleep and then 'coming to' again, having gone deep.

★ I imagine walking or lying under a clear sky gazing at the stars, and this mirrors awareness of my inner universe of beauty.

★ My centre is 'the ground of my being'. (Julian of Norwich)

★ I strive to sink down to 'the seed' within me, and out of this place I pray that I'll feel an upsurge of a new birth of life in me. I seek to be awakened, aflame with loving intention to manifest Spirit in my life in all its glory.

★ My centre is my rock of security in God.

★ I abide in God and God abides in me. I can rest into that.

★ My centre is a living fountain from which I may drink anytime.

★ I become aware of a state beyond words or 'where words come from'. I am engaged in an experiment with depth.

★ I'm aware that I have an enduring and unchanging part of myself, which is my sense of centre. Some call it a 'sense of soul' which is infused with connection to a Presence or Ultimate Reality, the ground or basic fabric of our existence that feels 'radically alive'. (Moss 1987) I'm then led into listening prayer.

Listening Prayer

Prayer is an energy that changes our hearts as we practise it, in that we become more loving. We also create more love, peace and joy in the world, as with the practice of mindfulness or centredness. When we 'return to ourselves' we are in touch with that energy and are then sending that out to others we pray for. We also have an innate longing to communicate with our Maker, who gave us life. We do this as naturally as breathing. We cry out for help, as a child does when in pain, hoping for our spiritual mother or father to answer our need. We listen in order to understand, like an infant who is unable to interpret the spoken word, yet knowing intuitively the heart's language of love.

As adults, in the silence of worship, we listen for guidance; for 'the still small voice' that Elijah heard. (1 Kings 19:13) We know that our prayers aren't always answered in the way we long for, but praying helps us to be connected both to the Divine centre within and to others we pray for.

People of all faiths and none are drawn to pray, to praise and celebrate the beauty of life. We have a power of Spirit within us that draws us to keep in contact with it, to abide in it; to be strengthened by it and that evokes compassion for all life in us. We too need our prayers as we try to discover what is the way of God for us and how can we live that. Prayer keeps our channel open to God and exercises our faith, which provides us with hope to understand those things that are hidden from us. We can use many ways into prayer.

When we do not know how to pray we are told that Spirit prays in us. Our wants and needs are known before we ourselves have expressed them. Prayer is a gift of Spirit yet our intentional practice is vital, so that we become 'collaborators with God'. (St. Paul)

"Who, then," we ask, "or what is this God that we pray to?"

GOD: giver and sustainer of life

★ I recall that when Moses asked God "Who are you?" the reply was "I am That I am." God just is!

★ As with other Quakers I've long since abandoned the image of God as an old man in the sky!

★ I pray to the Source of life that is within me and yet surrounds me, as present in all things created, good and bad.

★ God is form without form, Creator expressed also in chaos.

★ God is not matter, but Spirit; but Spirit that creates matter!

★ Prayer is an energy in contact with 'That' the unknowable, the "Other" yet felt presence, a subconscious communion with 'that of God' within me.

★ I pray to the numinous, Divine, unknowable and yet experienced force of power, energy, warmth, joy and light within and without.

★ God is not a person, nor a father or mother, but greater than I can envisage, a touchstone against which all other things can be judged. It is the power of love.

★ I worship what Wordsworth described as 'a Spirit that…rolls through all things'. This Spirit I feel is present within me, but also outside me, within other people and nature and connects me with them. It is a force, a mystery, which I cannot understand, which I'm content to live with and yet I seem to know and which seems to support and sustain us all.

★ I find helpful a Hindu prayer that I use: 'Show me thy face. Make me worthy of thy love O love Supreme and Beauty Absolute. Awaken in my being the flame of Truth and lead my inner and outer life to peace and love of Thee'.

★ There is an originating Power, a creative Spirit, a Source out of which all things come and in whose energy fields all things, all matter, all beings lie. My own spirit is in resonance with that Source, it is the Light within me, so precious and fragile that I can only honour it as Divine and sacred. To desecrate the Earth or kill another person is blasphemy to that sacramental Source.

LISTENING PRAYER: waiting for insight

★ When listening for guidance, I try to get my ego-self out of the way, so as to hear my inner voice of wisdom.

★ There are times when I recognise that something within me makes me uncomfortable. I then pray for clarity to find how to resolve it.

★ At times of pain I stand transparent before my Maker; feeling full of inadequacy. I use simple prayer, as a child: "Help me!"

★ I pray "Lead me. Show me the way" when I feel in the dark.

PRAYER OF THE FORSAKEN: fear of abandonment

★ I'm unsure as to whether I am heard! Then I pray for faith though mine is only 'as small as a mustard seed'. (Matt. 17:20) I recall that Martin Israel writes: 'Faith is an open, self-giving acceptance of an unknown, yet dimly glimpsed purpose that guides the flow of the cosmos...faith is consummated in two acts: an act of self-giving to God, however he/she/it may be conceived, and an act of commitment to follow the course Spirit indicates'.

★ I wonder whether I should pray if my prayers are not being answered. I understand that there are seasons in prayer; times of loss of a sense of God's presence called 'desolation' or 'the dark night of the soul'. A time of trial! I am forced to go deeper into my heart to discover what I really yearn for. American Quaker John Woolman, in the mid-1700s, had a dream whilst in fever, of having died. He had 'a vivid sense of his own will having died, of the life of Christ now in him.' I ask myself if I can die to my own will.

INTERCESSORY PRAYER: the advocate of Spirit

★ I pray for others, for their well-being and contentment.

★ When I pray for myself or others I gather love from within myself and combine it with the love that lies within another, to intercede for me ~ Jesus, Mary, a saint, Buddha, or another spiritual teacher.

★ As from a deep source within me, there can arise a groan or cry of pain, when my heart is moved in compassion for another, then I must pray. It is as if I am being 'acted upon'.

HEALING PRAYER: *loving others*

★ We all have to face death at some time and this increases my love for others. I pray for those facing death in war-torn countries as well as those in positions of power. I hold them 'in the Light' of God's love. Healing prayer then arises as I ask to be used as a conduit, through which God's love can flow: 'Make me an instrument of thy love'. (Francis of Assisi) I am 'prayed through'. (Thomas Kelly)

CONTEMPLATIVE PRAYER: *mystical union*

★ Hildegard of Bingen's prayer speaks for me. 'Am I a feather on your breath, a pebble on your ground; a mist dissolving in the All? You holy mystery, revealed in no-thing and in All, pulling me beyond myself into the true reality'.

★ Speak and I will hear. Call and I will answer. We are not strangers to one another. I live with you and you with me. But I forget! Forgive my forgetting! You are always with me. I eat you, drink you, walk with your strength. I see something of your glory in the sky and stars, in the water and sunlight, in the garden and on the hillside. I praise you, thank you, love you and surrender to you.

CELEBRATORY PRAYER: *the abundant life*

★ In the Meeting for Worship, the silence can pulse and throb with love and beauty as we are 'gathered' into the arms of Spirit.

★ I'm full of gratitude for the gift of life, the beauty of the world and the lovingness I receive. Joy moves me to prayer through song or dance like the Sufi whirling dervishes. Composers, writers and artists show their adoration through their art. My life is blessed!

SACRAMENTAL PRAYER: *blessed gifts*

★ We say grace before meals, thankful to the eternal Giver.

★ I find that God is revealed through the physical and the visible as in nature. But P.T. Forsyth writes 'True sacrament is holy personality'.

★ I pray 'to become a mirror in which…the greatness of Life will be reflected'. (Dag Hammarskjold)

Entering Light

'We are sons and daughters of the darkness and of the light'. (John O'Donohue) Our bodies were first formed in the darkness of the womb. With birth, our first journey was from darkness to light. Every thought we have is a flint moment, a spark of light from our inner darkness. 'Creativity awakens at this primal threshold where light and darkness test and bless each other'. Light is seen as the mother of life in the Celtic tradition. (John O'Donohue)

In the Bible story of Genesis, God said 'Let there be light' which heralded the creation of the cosmos out of chaos. We too may seek to be transformed, renewed. The physical light and the spiritual Light are used interchangeably as they inform each other in our understanding of creation and spirituality.

In the gathered Meeting for Worship, Light is seen as the presence of God in our midst, hence Quakers speak of "waiting in the Light" for guidance, as giving clarity or insight, or 'holding someone in the Light' when praying for them. Jesus is seen as 'the Light that enlightens' (John 1:9) and the Light of Love that intercedes, bringing healing. So Light is portrayed as a creative energy that is embodied in Jesus, but this Light of Love is also within each one of us. Others see Light as Life, which like light is freely given to all creation and like 'the unconditional love of God which, if we can accept it, we are able to radiate as Light to the world around us'. (Jim Pym)

Light is a universal symbol for the Divine in all world religions. Sometimes the Light is seen as a peaceful, gentle symbol, and at other times it is the fire that burns up the old self to allow the Divine to manifest. Sometimes the Light is personified, as with Christ the Light of the World, or the Buddha of Infinite Light in the Buddhist tradition.

JESUS: Light of the world

★ Jesus was the greatest prophet. His life and teachings are what I aspire to follow. He shows me how to love God, mankind, myself and how to live, how to pray and how to worship.

★ He used stories and metaphors to bring the Divine nature alive.

★ Jesus was a teacher and a revolutionary thinker whose programme, for the most part, is yet to be tried out!

★ Jesus suggested that we have a spiritual revolution in our hearts.

★ The man I know from the gospels is a man who in himself identified and revealed the reflection of God and illuminated the Light in others. He taught a new way of living, at the intersection of humanity with God – the possibility of heaven on Earth.

★ Jesus made himself transparent to the Light within him.

★ I believe in the Way of Jesus, not in worshipping Jesus.

★ A mentor, guide, friend, shepherd, healer, teacher, counsellor, inspirer, an example, a wonder; that of God manifest in human form. In all he did and was, he shows me how to live and how to suffer and to die with surrender and still to trust in Divine love.

CHRIST: the god-form in all

★ I understand that Christ, Krishna, Buddha are examples of 'god-forms' in all people's consciousness, from time's beginning.

★ I note that Jim Pym writes:

> The Light is also the Guide when it assumes a personal aspect for us. It is the Inner Teacher or Christ in us. The Light enables us to see the Way (another synonym for Christ) and follow the Way which is the right one for us in harmony with God's will. This Light is essentially loving but can be quite uncompromising in showing us where we have gone wrong.

★ I call myself a Quaker Christian and try to follow the teachings of Jesus Christ, as his disciples did, rather than putting an image of him on an altar to worship.

★ Jesus came to share his Light with us, that was of God and that is continually being revealed and is always present to be discovered.

WAITING IN THE LIGHT: *until the way opens*

★ Three hundred years ago Quakers were called 'Children of the Light'. They lived to radiate God's Light of love to all.

★ The Light can reveal my wounds and heal me with loving balm.

★ I stand in the Light naked, exposed and vulnerable, known to my Maker who conceived me. Where will I be led? It may be to the gas chamber, through darkness! In death I shall enter the Light.

★ I listen to the Light for understanding in my heart of how to be, praying that the Light will show me.

★ I get bright ideas, like meteorites shooting through my imagination. Should I act on them? I hold them in the Light.

★ I read that Pierre Lacout, who was a Carmelite, then later became a Quaker in Switzerland, discovered that 'In silence which is active, the Inner Light begins to glow – a tiny spark'.

★ To lead myself into stillness, I favour observing my breath's rise and fall for a time, then letting go, as I listen to the Light.

★ In my experience prayer is a pathway into entering the Light. Another way is through the practice of meditation, which I find prepares me for Meeting for Worship. They are ways of helping me to go deeper into the silence and to help me lose my sense of self or of separateness from the 'Other', and to experience the joy of Oneness, Union, and Bliss.

MEDITATION: *steadying the mind*

★ As I understand it, the aim of this practice is to reflect, contemplate, and to stay in the silence, so as to go deeper into union with the Divine. It is a method I use to help my individual spiritual development and towards self-realisation. I practise by myself or with a group. There are many ways I can be led into meditation: through chanting, visualising an image, using a mantra, a Bible passage, or a walking meditation to help me focus. The practice has a similar intent to Meeting for Worship, but differs, in that Quakers in the silence are all in communion together with the 'Presence in the Midst' which may inspire spoken ministry.

★ I regularly practise the Experiment with Light meditation with others. It involves following steps in centring down, to help us go deeper into the Light. Rex Ambler discovered that similar steps were used by Quakers in past centuries. This practice often reveals something that is troubling my conscience, or an unidentified joy. I can then gain the insight that Light reveals, for how the matter can be attended to and, if necessary, healed. It's a similar process to the 'Examen' exercise used in monastic traditions.

MYSTICAL CONTEMPLATION: *Light as transforming*

★ I have discovered that the mystics of all traditions have the ability to awaken the Light in others by recognising that it is there, in all creation. Many mystics practise meditation or contemplative prayer which Patrica Loring describes as 'the name given to the still, listening, nonverbal prayer in which we intentionally dispose ourselves to be receptive to God, either in conscious awareness of whatever is present or in openness to transformation in the depths of our being beyond consciousness'. We move to a universal centring or openness that is beyond our control and sometimes beyond our consciousness.

★ My understanding of the mystery of the Trinity, as a Quaker, is that 'I stand in awe and reverence of the Father. I love the Son. I unite myself with the Spirit'. I don't use those images in a literal sense, but symbolically, as demonstrating unconstrained love.

★ I feel in the presence of the Divine One indwelling in me and in all those worshipping with me.

★ I sometimes feel flooded with grace.

★ I feel tenderised and opened to joy and sorrow.

★ I enter a living stream of power and love.

★ I wish to be transformed in the furnace of God's love.

★ I pray: 'For God alone my soul waits in silence'. (Psalm 62:1)

★ When in 'union with God, will, memory and understanding are suspended' wrote Teresa of Avila. Can I experience this?

★ I would like to be in this world but not of it.

Knowing Promptings

In the seventeenth century Quakers knew well the call of the Inward Teacher in their hearts. Their letters, journals, books and pamphlets still inspire us today. They also spoke from the heart in Meetings for Worship, many times quaking physically (which led to the use of the name 'Quakers'). Words of encouragement were given to those members suffering from persecution for practising their faith. Their vocal ministry was frequently inspirational.

Today we need to listen for, hear and respond to what Spirit calls us to do or say as we search for the promptings of love and truth. As George Fox suggests, we 'wait in the Light' and examine our consciences. We know when we act with love or without it. The truth can be unpalatable, but we are led to know what we need to know, for "Truth is outside time..." Fox said. How then to act?

> When we receive the call it can be subtle. It can take time to decipher, like walking from bright sunlight into a darkened room. We need to prepare ourselves to be ready to hear, using such practices as prayer, meditation, spiritual reading, and whatever other spiritual disciplines we have found fruitful. (Patience Schenck)

Then we must do what we must, and surrender the outcome. Discerning when to speak and when to be still, in daily life as in Meeting for Worship, is a matter of intuition, which includes the use of reason, but our hearts will show us how to attend to what Creative Spirit requires of us. We can ask ourselves: "Is my vocal ministry in the service of the Meeting?"

A genuine concern or leading laid upon us, won't go away until it is satisfied. A prompting is more a nudge to discern the movement of Spirit opening before us and guiding us to play our part in the Divine unfolding.

We need to be fully alive and mindful to the moment and to stay with it, as our co-operation, or lack of it, is part of the creation of the next instant. We can strive to cultivate a life of prayer and to live daily under Divine guidance. In the silence of the Meeting for Worship, we attentively listen for murmurings of Spirit. Responding to inward promptings involves obedience to a transcendent, yet utterly present, spiritual dynamism. From this source we may be led or pushed to speak in Meeting.

★ If I speak, I want it to be from my heart: my deepest centre.

★ The richest vocal ministry that I've ever experienced has been from a Friend, now terminally ill, about her harrowing experience. She spoke of "reaching a point of almost no return" and calling out, as did Jesus: "My God why hast thou forsaken me?" and the answer that came was that God does not remove the pain, but is in the pain. She found that insight very comforting and strengthening and I found her ministry quite awe-inspiring.

★ I've found that when Friends are living together, whether it's adults at Woodbrooke, an all-age Meeting-away weekend, a work camp, or young people at Junior Yearly Meeting, worship reaches depths very rare on a Sunday. Some of the most profound vocal ministry I've ever experienced has been with Friends really raw and open through the intense processes of public performance in theatre or concert hall.

★ I was moved to sing something in Meeting. I became self-conscious and stumbled. I then had to lose myself in Spirit again before I could continue.

★ I usually feel full of emotion when I speak in Meeting. It may not be eloquent, but it comes from the depths of me.

★ I have often felt very nervous when giving vocal ministry, but 'I haven't trembled' as the negro spiritual says, when thinking about the crucifixion, or quaked as Friends used to do.

★ Sometimes I find that I can be led to reconsider a matter that's been troubling me, because of vocal ministry in Meeting that stays with me as a truth that I needed to recognise.

★ Some ministry I've heard will stay with me for ever, like the time a Friend said "God also loves his son, the dictator!" She set me an example of compassion for all.

★ I've been prompted to speak in Meeting for Worship a number of times, but then I experienced a prompting not to speak. I was tempted to judge a mother who spent much time in settling her children into the silence. Often near the close of Meeting she would stand up and speak, and sometimes it was just what we needed to hear and at other times I thought not. I wondered whether to speak to her, but a loving Spirit prompted me not to! What may not have been useful ministry for me might well have 'spoken to' another!

★ I find it unhelpful when a Friend speaks for too long, intruding into the precious silence. I love ministry being received into the silence. I dislike it when another Friend speaks in answer to another's ministry as though Meeting for Worship was a debating forum. Sometimes someone speaks just as the elders are about to shake hands to close the Meeting, which is too late. It is as if they are not sensitive to the needs of the gathered Meeting.

★ Prepared reading can be helpful as a teaching ministry, but at another time not, as the Meeting for Worship is such a unique immediate experience of that day, time and place.

★ I hate 'social activism'-type ministry. It jars me. Worship is the wrong context for that. I call it 'soap box' ministry!

★ Once during worship I became aware of my discomfort at what I felt was a stuck situation in my Meeting. I was guided to suggest later to elders and overseers that we have a spiritual review and they agreed. The questions that were raised for discussion stirred people and this led to mutual promptings. Ways were found to bring new life to Meeting and to worship.

★ I love it when somebody prays out loud in Meeting. It lifts me!

★ I have found that I need to 'wait in patience', as George Fox suggests, for a prompting or some guidance, as often I am impatient to 'do' rather than to just 'be'.

★ Sometimes I feel overloaded and uncertain. I lay that into the silence of Meeting. Later fresh vision comes to me and I sigh, "Thank you!"

★ As an elder I sometimes feel led to offer, with sensitivity to the Meeting's state, some 'teaching' ministry through the reading of a Psalm or a passage from the Bible or , that might 'fulfil' the silence.

★ Wonderful ministry can be given by those holding the silence.

★ I often reflect on Meister Eckhart's teaching: 'The Father's speaking is his giving birth: the Son's hearing is his being born. We cannot serve this Word better than in stillness and silence: there we can hear it, and there too we will understand it aright – in the unknowing. To him who knows nothing it appears and reveals itself.'

★ What do I do when words come, as fragments, holding them in the Light to see where they take me, blossoming or withering as they will? They may rise within me and I feel drawn to stumble to my feet. Sometimes words tumble out like water from a mountain stream, catching something headlong; sometimes they come hewn from hard rock and fall with pieces too heavy to carry, they just lie there artificially...this is the way the world is. Sometimes a stone has been polished and I give it as a thing made with the elegance of a haiku; sometimes I ground myself in my tradition with wise words from small and large red books. I still quake, in the heart or gut, as I make my offering, be it ever so small; this I can say, but do I say it for all of us? Like ropes of sand, ministry holds together. Often I say "I hope" or "I promise..." or "I give thanks..." or "I pray...?" I confidently can speak of what I do not know, as my faith in Spirit bids me not always to be silent.

Bonding Community

Quakers have been known as Children of the Light, Friends in the Truth, a People of God, the Priesthood of all Believers, and at heart such claims still hold. Today we see ourselves as a company of both seekers and finders, disciples and friends, of the Spirit-led and the world-engaged.

Of all places, the Divine is most expressed in our relationships and, outside our groupings of intimate bondings, the Society can be an extended family. Its caring and tender way of going about its affairs, of helping each other up when we are ill or have fallen, is an inspiration that many Friends attempt to carry over into their places of work and community.

Yet we are normal, human people with conflicts and quarrels and often thrown in with those we would least want to live with, if given a choice. How we resolve those divisions and learn to live amicably alongside each other becomes the way of the Spirit. 'Love is the hardest lesson in Christianity; but for that reason it should be most our care to learn it'. (William Penn) We learn that small loving acts can help to generate the slow growth of love. Without creed and uniformity of belief we hold extraordinarily divergent views. Our aspiration is to embrace difference and find acceptance ourselves: to be who we are. Our hope is we might become a model for a loving, holding together of diversities.

The beginning of this community bonding spills from our worship ~ from ministry, afterwords, the shaking of hands, from news and notices, refreshments and socialising. They are each a threshold to the Life of the Meeting: the integration of children and young people, the sharing of committee responsibilities, having been nominated to them for our gifts and needs, to meetings for learning, social celebrations and our leadings to witness in the world. But what is evolving is a rare community: one founded in Spirit.

MAKING THE MOST OF SUNDAY: seizing the opportunity

★ *Afterword* Some years ago we picked up the idea of Afterword from a Woodbrooke weekend and after a precarious start it is now an integral part of our worship, helping newcomers feel at home. Around the end of the hour, when appropriate, an elder stands and briefly invites Friends in the manner of worship-sharing to tell us what they might have ministered, or reflect uncritically about what was ministered, or share a thought or spiritual quotation. Many speak who haven't the courage yet to minister and many have gained clearness about our Quaker ways and understandings. After about ten minutes or so, the shaking of hands then seems to bring us closer than before and, if the children have been present, they are fascinated by the conversation and have even taken part.

★ *Notices* When I was the Meeting's clerk I was determined to make the ritual of notices more of an event. We started a monthly bulletin, given out on the first Sunday of each month, with all the events, times and places on one side, and more news and reports on the other. So, apart from brief reminders, we had time for Friends to share news of celebrations and illnesses, speak to the allotted appeals and hear of an occasion in a lively way. I feel passionately that this bridging time between worship and socialising is of vital importance for the Meeting to feel its own identity.

★ *Refreshments* Ours is quite a big Meeting and it's often like Babel when notices finish! It can be overwhelming to newcomers, so we've developed a range of strategies with overseers, designated welcomers, as well as doorkeepers, to be aware of those who are new or standing apart or bewildered. We've found it can't be left to chance, but is a great opportunity to listen and get to know.

★ *Discussion lunches and breakfasts* I've been a Friend for over thirty years and wherever I've worshipped there's always been some sort of monthly discussion lunch, either bring-and-share or a picnic eat-your-own. Topics range every-which-way, from exploring testimonies to hot issues for the Society or the Meeting. In summer months rather than discuss we've gone for a walk together or had a picnic outside. I've also known pre-worship times for breakfast discussions; or half-hour worship-sharings on extracts from *Quaker Faith and Practice*; or even a monthly singing session.

CHILDREN AND WORSHIP: working for an all-age community

★ I've always been intrigued by silence. This goes way back to my first experiences in Meeting as a child. I relied on gazing out of the high windows at the trees outside to pass the time. I found I could just get my mind to 'hang' or 'hover', creating a space for 'something' to arrive. This wasn't difficult or odd to me, for it seemed to chime in with an 'inner silence', which I could feel at my core – it was as though two silences, inner and outer, were coming to-gether, recognising one another and finding harmony and meaning.

★ As a child I sat through Meeting for Worship as there was no children's class, with a book of *Stories of Jesus* that I could read so long as I didn't drop it or make a noise turning the pages. I looked at everyone's faces and wondered why everyone looked so worried. I decided that Meeting was where people brought their worries!

★ I'm involved in the children's groups and am always moved by our monthly children's Meeting to which some of the adults come. Children act as welcomers and elders and will have chosen what objects they want on the table. These can be tied in with the theme they will be exploring in a worship-sharing way, often about caring for the environment. On Christmas Day in our all-age programmed Meeting, they read all the Bible passages, followed by a silence, then the next carol; and some play instruments to join with the piano. Around midsummer the children are central to another all-age Meeting based around what the groups have been working on for the last couple of months. One year it was *Pilgrim's Progress* with adult Friends being all manner of goodies and baddies on the journey; other years the story of early Friends or John Woolman or Elizabeth Fry were shared together. The Meetings are noisier than many, but there's engagement and joy.

MEETINGS FOR LEARNING: tools for deepening worship

★ Over the years I've grown in confidence with group facilitation skills. At first I was terrified when asked to run a session, but the encouragement of Friends was a tonic and I had another go. In a do-it-yourself faith, the Quaker way is that everyone plays a part, and with the guidance of more experienced Friends it's soon possible to run evenings exploring a study pack, like *Hearts and Minds Prepared* or the *Testimonies Toolkit*.

★ I've found that one of the best ways of Friends finding out about each other is to run an evening series on 'my life'. Talking for half an hour about yourself, then answering questions in a sympathetic group and seeing them open out the discussion into important matters for reflection is really rewarding.

★ Studying the Bible always seemed to divide us more than unite us, everyone holding such different views. But we came across the *Friendly Bible Study* by Joanne and Larry Spears, published by Friends General Conference in America. It's a way of looking at texts through our own experience and not through academic theories and scholastic quibbling. We've gone deep this way. One memorable exploration spent six months on the Lord's Prayer.

★ Our elders take it in turns, often working with another member of the Meeting, to be responsible for a series of five or six evening sessions on a topic that Friends have requested at our annual planning discussion lunch. They may be held in the Meeting House or in somebody's home and usually attract between six to twelve. Different Friends facilitate each evening, so that the homework is not too onerous for anyone. Anything goes: from different early Friends, medieval mystics, Quaker testimonies, Swarthmore Lectures, to our faith in action, 'my job', and 'books that have changed me'. At times we've examined one book, like Matthew Fox's *Original Blessing*, taking one chapter a session. We always end up knowing more about each other than the topic and often they've led to some kind of personal or Meeting action.

Following Leadings

Quaker worship and Quaker witness have been intertwined from our very beginnings. The Light in our hearts will reveal personal need and social need. It prompts, nudges, urges, propels us into action, if we are responsive to it. Worship tenderises the spirit within us; it nurtures the ground of our being. Then in our daily life, each of us responds to a particular need in a particular way; we are moved and feel led to do something about it. Our tradition points the way. In the lives and journals of Friends such as George Fox, John Woolman and Elizabeth Fry we are shown 'patterns and examples' of how the seed of an idea springs; how it will be long lived-with and persists; how it is tested within, to see if it is just inflation, pride or will; and tested without, amongst intimate others, our spiritual guides, our local and wider Quaker Meetings.

Here it is often thwarted and discouraged, but if the leading is authentic then teeth are gritted, often loyal companions found, the Spirit is sought for empowerment, and the first tentative, experimental action is taken. The nature of the response sees collapse and withering away, or a green shoot of encouragement. This may grow into a personal undertaking; or a project for our Meeting; or new work for a Quaker charity to witness in the world; or into a concern that is taken up by the whole Society. It will need dedication and stickability, often 'one per cent inspiration and ninety nine per cent perspiration', but when fired by Spirit and not for personal gain or glory there will be a blessedness of a true leading's grace and all those involved will know deep transformation.

A LEADING WITHIN A FAMILY: offering home to a refugee
I was led to foster a Vietnamese teenager. I was a single mother of three and my eldest son had recently gone to university. In 1979 the 'boat people' arrived in Britain in the thousands, fleeing the war

in Vietnam. I had a job for a few years helping families resettle in South East England for the British Refugee Council. On my visits I heard of a thirteen-year-old boy living at a residential children's home in Swindon without a family. None of the other families would foster him as they knew nothing about his background. He spoke little English, was teased by others at the Home and was clearly unhappy there. He got into quarrels with the children and staff and was labelled 'unruly'. I spoke to his social worker and no options seemed available to rehouse him.

I was moved by his plight and sought to discern what to do, and felt a strong leading to foster him myself. I prayed that an alternative could be found, but none appeared. I then felt, despite my uncertainty at the work involved and the disruption to my family life, that I must offer this to him. I spoke to my two teenage children and they were very generous, agreeing that they would still have the privacy of their own bedrooms and Kim could sleep on the put-u-up in the sitting room. I invited Kim to come and stay for a week and to see how we all got on. He stayed for several years, until he was able to be reunited with his family who had fled to America. It was the testing of this leading with my children, the social worker and my Quaker spiritual director that helped me discern whether this was what Spirit required of me: for I felt I was led or driven to do it by the movement of my concern.

WITHIN A LOCAL MEETING: witnessing for peace

In my experience a leading is a direction that may first come when I allow myself to be open and listening. Then it needs reflection and testing. After 9/11, Friends in my Meeting decided to hold regular evening worship Meetings to pray for peace. At first we came with sadness and anger. We had no plans for witness; we wanted to be together and hold our concerns in the Light. We spoke about our feelings, how war destroys the Spirit in victims and perpetrators. I felt we connected to 'love and truth in our hearts'. From there it became clear that we wished to state publicly the Quaker faith that each person is a precious child of God ~ and we wanted to witness that belief in a way that was entirely congruent with it. We wished to say "no" to war by holding out our hands and connecting with people.

After each Meeting, we reflected in worship-sharing, which helped us discern how to take up our leadings. Within the group we had wide experience from campaigning to counselling, so had a sense of what was practical. As there were several ideas, we decided to support one another in our complementary directions. Together we organised silent vigils before the peace demonstrations in central London, our intention being to offer time for listening and stillness as a statement of our values and as prayerful preparation before the marches. I believe we were led in the stillness of the Meeting to witness as we did. With compassion and experience as guides, we received the clarity and energy to act in faith.

WITHIN A QUAKER CHARITY: responding to social need

My leadings have been both to behave towards others and my environment in a particular way and to undertake specific work. By being led I mean 'drawn towards' actions that express an inner conviction. This is a subtle process, not often a conscious one, requiring a degree of openness, combinations of circumstance, a vision of an outcome or goal, trust in yourself and others, conviction, communication and application. These leadings have been 'of God' where they have expressed the spirit that Jesus and others have brought to our common life.

For example, I was managing a city farm, a most varied and enjoyable job, when I was asked to help an old Quaker organisation that was in difficulty. It had been declining for years; there was one remaining staff member running a project whose lease and funding were three months from finishing, and relations with its historic funder were now troubled. They needed a manager at a basic wage, I had a young family and mortgage, but the organisation might fold in months.

A move would be very risky but it touched a chord – the project was tackling poverty and that appeared a higher purpose. I would have less time than normally needed to raise money and save the venture and I'd be on my own. I took a leap of faith and switched jobs. Amazingly I found both a local trust that could decide on a significant grant quickly; a rare circumstance, and a premises I could rent. The project was saved and in later years was giving twenty young people a year their first paid work. With hard work and discernment I also started other undertakings and left it all in a healthy and respected state, with over 2000 people in new housing and employment, and more than that not having suffered debt.

WITHIN AN AREA MEETING: the evolution of a national concern
Six of us met for five years as mutual support in our Quaker work, often lamenting that if we sat on the London Eye and looked out over one of the largest cities in the world, there would only be a handful of Quakers detectable down below. Yet there was a growing spiritual search afoot and the times threatened crisis ahead. We approached our Area Meeting with an outreach project; were warmly received as the issue spoke to other Friends as well; and within months were started on six months preparation to launch Quaker Quest in Friends House for a year during 2002, the Quaker 350th anniversary. Every Monday night for that year the twelve of us, and soon many others, spoke to the public about our faith and our practice, and amazingly about twenty seekers attended each time. After eight years it continues. Other meetings started copying the pattern of a repeated cycle of sessions addressed by different Friends, which spurred the launching of a Travelling Team to work throughout Britain Yearly Meeting. Friends in over a hundred local meetings have now initiated their own projects, often repeating them annually. Workshops have been run in Europe, Australia, Africa and America; Meeting for Sufferings has been reported to; a national network responds and supports; and new 'nurturing newcomers' work develops. The team feels profoundly Spirit-led.